Learning Self-Therapy Through Writing

an experience in Creative Journaling

by Dr. Nathaniel Gadsden

Biography by Kelly Sloane Britt

Learning Self-Therapy Through Writing an experience in Creative Journaling

This manual is not intended to take the place of a professional counselor or therapist. It is the recommendation of the author that this manual is used only as a guide by the reader. The author conducts workshops on the use of this manual. For more information visit www.upublish.com/books/gadsden.htm

Published by Universal Publishers / uPUBLISH.com
USA • 2000

ISBN: 1-58112-703-0

www.upublish.com/books/gadsden.htm

Acknowledgments

Special thanks to Marsha Bryant owner of M. Bryant Concepts for her writing and development contributions to this project. She has the magic touch.

(M. Bryant Concepts - 1/888-445-0445)

Special thanks to Julie Clay of Signal Graphics Printing for her layout and cover design of this project. There is none better.

(Signal Graphics Printing 717/697-6333)

Special thanks to Patricia Gadsden, my wife, for her encouragement and love.

(P. Gadsden - Life Esteem 717/233-7611)

This work was inspired by...

Steven M. Cunningham, Author
Back from the Gutter

Gordon Graham, Author
Breaking Barriers

Many thanks also to...

Kent Groff,
Oasis Ministries

Reverend Barbara Derrickson,
Chaplain, York Hospital, PA

About the Author
by Kelly Sloane Britt

Nathaniel Gadsden wears many hats. Poet, counselor, father, Reverend, husband, teacher, doctor of philosophy. During a period in America when intellectualism tends to breed classism and inaccessibility, Nate successfully challenges and defeats such stereotypes. While he is accomplished in many arenas, his foundation remains spiritual and his door is always open. With a wealth of knowledge and experience to call his own, Nate Gadsden is ever prepared to share his wealth while remaining a perpetual student of life.

Comparable to the custom of village poets and storytellers in traditional African cultures, years ago a tradition was initiated in his Grandmother's living room. Nate recognized at an early age that each member of his family migrated to his Grandmother's home for counsel and words of advice. He realized that while his Grandmother was not well educated by today's standards, the wealth of her experience and her willingness to share her journey with others was priceless. This was Nate's first confirmation that experience was a most credible teacher.

While still a youth, Nate became aware of how beautiful and tragic and wondrous the journey of life is. Born and raised in Harrisburg, Pennsylvania, he learned first hand the realities of the welfare system, the single parent household and the devastation of alcoholism. While he often found himself grief stricken by his circumstances and painfully aware of life's ironies, Nate never felt defeated. On the contrary, he began to question everything and everyone and embarked on a journey in search of his own voice.

During his high school years, Nate embraced the value of community. His extended family willfully accepted the task of providing he and his brother with a spiritual and healthy living environment. He participated in organized sports and upon entering college, formed the first of many communities he would create.

Nate's awareness of his immediate surroundings as well as the enormous change that was occurring in his life and in America fostered a need for him to begin documenting his journey. He was energized by the documents and orators of the civil rights and black pride movements. He was inspired by the voices of the Last Poets and Gil Scott Herion captured on vinyl. The power and relevance of the written and spoken word intrigued him.

Poetry became a logical outlet for Nate as it allowed him to document the realities of the journey of his while creating a forum for addressing those realities. Strangers and friends gather not only to hear the poet speak but to hear the poet capture pain and hope and promise in words. The feeling can be communal; the listener's eyes may close or the head rocks to and fro and then, "yes!". For a moment, one individual's reality is personified or perhaps enlightened by another. In the oral tradition, Nate discovered that poetry breeds community and, in the poetic sense of the word, he also found home.

As an orator, Nate commands an amazingly humble yet motivational, compelling and accessible presence. Trite references or cliches are not permitted. When he speaks, one feels that truth, light, empathy, clarity, and vision are at play. All the makings of healthy and spirited community.

A living testament to Dr. Gadsden's understanding that arts breed community, compassion and awareness, the small extended family of the Writers Wordshop. The Wordshop has become a forum that isn't consumed with racial, class or ethical issues. It is, however, a forum for exploring such issues. Devoid of traditional formulas for educational outlets, the Writers Wordshop is a venue that promotes dialogue beyond elocution and transcends the partitions of the Neighborhood Community Center. Issues, realities, myths, statistics, and rhetoric are internalized, questioned, and thoroughly examined. Slowly undressed and artfully crafted, Nate facilitates the creation of a new life line from the mind to pen to paper. A new community.

With all of the hats that Nate elects to wear in a given day, community and awareness remain. He generously continues the tradition his Grandmother initiated years ago with his immediate family and an extended family of communities he has either created, cultivated or nurtured. Whether at work in the community at the Neighborhood Center, the Writers Wordshop, Christ Community Outreach Church or in counsel with troubled foster children or hospice patients, Nate considers himself a life long student of human behavior. While his experience and education permit him to engage professionally in efforts toward improving the lives of others, he is ever aware of the priceless gift he receives when granted the opportunity to engage in such an exchange.

Recently, Nate presented poetry at a Pennsylvania university. After his reading, an excited student told Nate of how thrilling the reading was and that the students needed him there. He was flattered to learn that by sharing his experience, the student felt such a tremendous amount of kinship. After considering the matter further, he laughed out loud. "They thought they needed me? I needed them!" His ability and need to keep one foot in the community, whether that community is the "hood" or the academy, is surely one of his greatest assets.

In 1998, undoubtedly with the increased public awareness of the value of poetry, Nate was appointed Poet Laureate of the City of Harrisburg in 1998. A new hat. Nate's understanding of the diversity of human kind and his ability to weave in and out of the intricate social confines of American society will surely prove beneficial in this arena. Perhaps his awareness of the similarities that exist within all humankind and his ability to transcend judgment will help foster a greater sense of community in the City of Harrisburg and the Central Pennsylvania region.

Poet, counselor, father, Reverend, husband, teacher, doctor of philosophy. Many hats. One simple message. There is always more to learn, see, feel and experience if one is willing to share.

We said Amen - For the word had been spoken.
We broke hands - and I did not speak.
We broke hands - and I did not speak.
I was honored.
I was honored.
I gave witness to the work - and that was enough."

Excerpt from The Journey
Dr. Nathaniel J. Gadsden

Table of Contents

Do you know that you are the only one of you? You are absolutely unique. There is no one like you. **You** are the original article. God only made **one,** and you are **it.**

Think what this means! You are a completely in charge of your own life. **You** determine what happens to **you** by being true to that self which you really are. Shakespeare said, "To thine own self be true, and it must follow as the night the day, thou cannot then be false to any man."

So be yourself today! The world is waiting for **you!** Do what you have to do, joyously and with all your heart!

Anonymous

OVERVIEW
Learning Self-Therapy Through Writing

The multifaceted model for this course is designed to serve as a guide to help you get safely off the emotional merry-go-round that often keeps people 'stuck' ~ with writing as the primary tool for change. The imagery of poetry, the creativity of story-writing, and the exploration of feelings through journaling are pathways toward a foundation for self-discovery. As you engage the written word throughout the *Learning Self-Therapy Through Writing* series, you will develop effective methods to not only recognize feelings such as anger, pain, abandonment, grief and even happiness ~ you will also learn to define, examine and manage those and other feelings!

Learning to achieve emotional stability is often quite a precarious balancing act. Emotions can be overwhelming. Unchecked and unmanaged, emotions can render us incapable of successfully functioning day-to-day. Faced with painful occurrences of the present, fears about the future, and unresolved issues from the past, one can begin to feel 'stuck'. Or, to coin an old phrase, one may have the sense of being "up the creek without a paddle". But congratulations! You have made the decision to claim a more harmonious life! You are now ready to begin the revealing journey that takes you far, far away from the place we will call ~~~

Someday Isle.

The Model

Someday Isle is not the place you want to be! As the model for this series, 'Someday Isle' translates to "Someday I'll".

How often do you proclaim to yourself, "Someday I'll do this" or "Someday I'll do that"? Most of us unconsciously set ourselves up for defeat. We do so by thinking and uttering these self-fulfilling prophecies which thwart progress, contentment and success. *Learning Self-Therapy Through Writing* sets the stage and prepares you to realize the potential within. This series will also empower you with the skills necessary to direct the course of your life ~ for the rest of your life!

HOW IT WORKS

IT WORKS BEST WHEN YOU WORK AT IT! As you plan your getaway from Someday I'll, you will encounter four bridges. These are the Bridges of **I AM ~ I CAN ~ I WANT TO ~ I'LL DO IT TODAY**! *Learning Self-Therapy Through Writing* provides clear guidelines and encourages expeditious timelines. For your journey, several tools are required. They include pen and paper, your workbooks and journal, a willingness to do the work, and an open mind. The activities include creative writing, self-examination, and mutual sharing with others who have also chosen to cease dwelling on Someday I'll. At times you may feel the journey is too rocky and the waves are too steep. Yet as you trek through the pages that follow, you will internalize that YOU are in charge of your life. Learning Self-Therapy Through Writing is a lifelong mission toward the fulfillment of personal freedom and happiness!

And now, your journey begins.

Introduction to
Learning Self-Therapy Through Writing

Who Am I? What Is Most Important To Me? These are the questions we seldom ask, although throughout our lives, we strive and struggle to find out who we are to make sense of our existence. The search can be a happy exploration or a painful struggle – often both. Seeking understanding of our sometimes puzzling thoughts and feelings, we typically try to assemble the many bits of our behavior to somehow make a whole. And while this is going on, we frequently lose ourselves in the defenses we have so carefully set up to keep us from seeing ourselves and keep us from being ourselves! What we are seeking is ~ identity.

When we are unclear and unsure about our own identity, feelings of insecurity, self-defeating thinking, and the ability to sort out emotions becomes progressively skewed. When we are unclear and unsure about our identity, it is difficult to make choices based on true needs and desires, or even to realize options and alternatives. Clearly, establishing identity is the starting point toward self-examination – and ultimately, the ability and know-how to acknowledge and address the issues which affect our lives.

 *Exercise*

1.　Write a brief paragraph answering the question: "Who am I?"

2.　Write a brief paragraph answering the question: "What is most important to me?"

MY DECLARATION OF SELF-ESTEEM

I am me.

I was uniquely created by God. There's not another human being in the whole world like me–I have my very own fingerprints and I have my very own thoughts. I was not stamped out of a mold like a Coca-Cola top to be the duplicate of another.

I own all of me–my body, and I can do with it what I choose; my mind, and all of its thoughts and ideas; my feelings, whether joyful or painful.

I own my ideals, my dreams, my hopes, my fantasies, my fears.

I reserve the right to think and feel differently from others and will grant to others their right to thoughts and feelings not identical with my own.

I reserve the right to think and feel differently from others and will grant to others their right to thoughts and feelings not identical with my own.

I own all my triumphs and successes. I own also all my failures and mistakes. I am the cause of what I do and am responsible for my own behavior. I will permit myself to be imperfect. When I make mistakes or fail, I will know that **I** am not the failure–I am still O.K.–and I will discard some parts of me that were unfitting and will try new ways.

I will laugh freely and loudly at myself–a healthy self-affirmation.

I will have fun living inside my skin.

I will remember that the door to everybody's life needs this sign: Honor Thyself

I have value and worth.

I am me, and I am O.K.

ANONYMOUS

SELF IMAGE
SELF IMAGE

You have written about your self image ~ who you think you are, and what things matter to you most. This should have provided some insight into fundamental notions of your 'self'. While it is important to develop your own sense of self, it is also relevant to analyze why you think of yourself as you do.

When reviewing your past, what are the most troublesome issues you believe prevent you from becoming the person you desire to be? For instance, as a student in middle and high school, you may have developed serious problems with procrastination over the years that were never checked. A result could be that you are now puzzled as to why you never seem to complete assignments – at least not on time. Or, maybe you felt someone close to you had little faith in you becoming successful and often told you so. They may have put you down. A result may be that today, you find you have low self esteem. It is important to learn to examine why we develop other-than-positive self images.

Only through touching the root cause are we able to hope for and work toward change. Indeed, you can re-write the script and begin to see yourself as you want to be, and then make the life-changes to help you reach that goal! You can take charge!

The following exercise is designed to help you develop insights as to why you see yourself the ways you do:

 *Exercise*

Recollect the images you had of yourself as a child; as an adolescent; as a teenager. It is important to be frank and honest with yourself. Try to use 'one-word' descriptions and very brief phrases.

A.   Childhood image ~

quiet, shy, "inside the lines"

B.   Adolescent image ~

awkward & confused, painfully unhappy

C.   Teenage image ~

extremely happy, in love with life, exuberant, excitable, quick to form strong bonds with people.

D.   Present image ~

Unfulfilled.

E.   How do I want to see myself in five years?

F.   How would I like to view myself in ten years?

 *Exercise*

Write your autobiography. *(Use only the front and back of this page.)*

Discussion Questions
About Your Autobiography

1. What part of your autobiography was the most fun to write about?

2. What part was the most difficult to write about?

3. Did you write about parts of your life from your early childhood?

4. Did you include your achievements in your autobiography?

5. Did you include any failures in your autobiography?

6. What is the one thing you left out of your brief autobiography?

Someday I'll.....

Now that you have begun to consider your self image, and defined who you are and what is important to you, let's go a step further. It is time to approach the first Bridge of Someday I'll...***The Bridge of I AM***.

This exercise is designed to further help you identify who you really believe yourself to be ~ and how you really feel about yourself. In an earlier exercise, you wrote about "Who am I?" and "What is most important to me?"

Now, try and list the things about yourself that you find puzzling or even mysterious ~ what drives you to do the things you do. For instance, in relationships, you may express feelings you know aren't true and wonder why. Or, you find yourself saying 'YES' when asked to do something and you really want to say 'NO'.

Do you often make decisions you know are not in your own best interest? Do you believe you consistently sacrifice your own wishes and desires to do what someone else wants you to do? Could you be a 'people pleaser'?

This exercise does not refer to those necessary and required commitments such as work or school, or the typical give-and-take required of committed relationships. No, it refers to circumstances in which you had - or have - a choice, and made decisions you later regretted. While we all do this occasionally, 'people pleasers' habitually go out of their way, with the hope that others will like them more. One result is that you then feel put-upon, unhappy with yourself, and resentful toward the person or circumstance.

 *Exercise*

1.   Do I often say things to people that I do not feel or that I do not mean? Give three brief examples where your behavior has fit these circumstances.

2.   Think for a minute. How did you feel in those scenarios? In brief phrases, list the feelings you had at the moment you were being dishonest with yourself. Contrast those feelings with how you felt sometime later about having been dishonest with yourself.

3.   *Respond:* Why did I choose to behave in those ways? What was / is the payoff? In brief phrases, I will list how I benefited from misrepresenting my true feelings.

FRIENDSHIP

There is nothing in this whole world, Lord, like having one true, enjoyable, understanding friend. No one is ever so lonely that he doesn't have a friend. To find one, all you have to do is go out and help somebody. Now and then say to a friend, "I love you." Those words weren't meant only for sweethearts. They are just as significant, beautiful and life-enhancing when said to a dear friend. A true test of friendship: If you died, which of your friends would you trust to clean out your drawers? When I talk, my friend listens. When my friend talks, I listen. That's one of the reasons we're friends. Friends are like bracelet charms. If you truly love and enjoy your friends, they are part of the golden circle that makes life good. If you want more friends, smile more! I've never known anyone who smiled a lot who didn't have a lot of friends. Friends are too precious to lose–even when they disappoint us. Lord, help me to forgive this friend–it is only because I need and love her. (And because I'd want her to forgive me!) Friends are worth forgiving. The heart has many doors, of which friendship is but one. Don't be too quick to bolt them.

Anonymous

The bridge of I AM

The Bridge of I AM is where you come to grips with who you are, and how you feel about yourself. It is the fundamental arena in which beliefs about 'self' are created and nurtured. To identify what "I AM" means is step one toward becoming the person you desire to be. It is the area in which you discover why you think of yourself as you do, and what things over your lifetime have brought you to your conclusions.

The importance of the self-concept in an individual goes far beyond providing a basis for one's reality. The self image begins to form very early in life. In infancy, we constantly explore ourselves and the world around us. We learn what is 'me' and what is 'not me' and discover we are a separate being. We learn to respond to our own name and acquire a sense of our own identity.

As we grow, we develop an increasingly complex and sophisticated image of who we are. Our self image is heavily influenced by certain 'significant others' ~ the persons with whom we are in close interaction. In early years, these influential persons almost certainly include our parents / caregivers, siblings, and other family members. Later, neighbors, teachers and schoolmates help shape our images of ourselves.

In our interaction with these significant others we come, to a large extent, to see ourselves as others see us. We learn from others' reactions what our qualities are and the value or worth attached to these qualities. We learn the areas of endeavor in which we do well and those in which we do poorly. We learn how competent, how attractive, how acceptable, how lovable we are.

With increasing age, we become less vulnerable to others' opinions about us. We pay less attention to the external forces of our environment. We arrive at a firmer sense of self that is less open to challenge and change because of what others seem to determine about who and what we are. Still, those early reactions regarding our personal worth and personal value tend to stick in the sub-conscious. Therefore, we also may become more adept at masking undesirable personal qualities and hide them from ourselves as well as from others ~ until we become strangers to ourselves and barely know who we are.

Some psychologists believe that the basic human force or tendency is about our striving to maintain and enhance the concept of 'self'. Yet others in the field of human behavior do not assign the same preeminence to the self image ~ that the self image is not what drives our thoughts, attitudes, feelings and actions. No matter which school of thought you accept, we probably would all agree on one thing; that when an individual has a solid notion of who he thinks he is and why, it is easier to understand present behavior, relate the present to the past, and even make some predictions about the future. To make the changes you want to see in yourself, it is first necessary that you have a clear picture of who you are!

The following exercise is designed to help you determine whether and how your present self image is anchored. Is your image of yourself tied to institutionalized roles and statuses? How mutable (changeable, variable, alterable) do you believe your self image to be, if at all? Are you a puzzle to yourself?

Before starting this exercise, review the workbook page titled: Writing Poetry: Some Basic Techniques. It is intended to provide some fundamental methods for developing writing skills, with a focus on poetry. It will also stimulate the ability to make close observations, and find new and unusual relationships among things in the world. This includes making connections between your world and YOU!

WRITING POETRY: SOME BASIC TECHNIQUES

Poetry is the most concise and powerful form of discourse, and writing poetry can be a tremendous help in further developing language and thinking skills. It requires focus, encourages the writer to think about feeling and meaning, and aids in learning to articulate abstract ideas. Poetry guides us to listen to language and choose words and phrases with care. *Learning Self-Therapy Through Writing* presents ideal methods of linking one's self with all things. By verbalizing feelings and thoughts ~ and mirroring them back to one's self ~ the stage is set for self-discovery, acceptance, healing, integration, and change where desirable.

The reading and writing of poetry are inseparable. In *Learning Self-Therapy Through Writing,* sharing is an essential ingredient, although you alone must determine what is appropriate for your private journal – which will be discussed later. You may share with an entire class, or with a small group. You may share with your facilitator. The willingness to share your strengths and weaknesses through the written word provides several bonuses. A few of them are listed:

1. Talking to others about issues that impact your life can result in valuable feedback. You get fresh perspectives, and new ways of viewing things.

2. Verbalizing your own challenges often triggers others to recall similar experiences, allowing you to know that you are not alone, that others have been there!

3. Expressing your feelings through poetry, word association, and other writing styles and techniques increases your ability to more concisely define emotions.

4. Logging your thoughts through journaling is a powerful way to measure changes and similarities in your thinking, attitudes and behaviors over periods of time.

5. Learning to develop ideas through writing is empowering. Writing improves communication skills and stimulates self-expression with others ~ and with yourself!

POETIC TECHNIQUES

Writing about one's self is often considered one of the most difficult of all writing tasks. As you continue *Learning Self-Therapy Through Writing,* it will be helpful to also develop methods of incorporating language that defines exactly what you want to say ~ even though what you want to say may be symbolic, or may involve the use of imagery. Several techniques are incorporated in the poem below. Try to visualize the words you read in the poem by Judith Steinbergh, called *Fireflies*. Steinbergh says she wrote the poem while sitting in a field in Maine.

Fireflies

Cool green fireflies

flit over the Maine meadow

dark then lit.

They stitch the summer night

with pale threads of light.

Fireflies rise

out of grass

like hundreds of

green eyes blinking

linking us

to the distant

stars.

Focusing Questions

We begin with sense imagery.

a. Which sense does the poet focus on?

   Almost entirely on sight.

b. Can you hear some examples of alliteration?

   Fireflies flit.   Maine meadow.

c. Which words rhyme exactly?

   Flit and lit   Night and light.   Blinking and linking.

d. Which words sound similar but do not rhyme exactly?

   Lit and Stitch.   Dark and Stars.

e. What comparisons can you find?

   The simile of fireflies rising like hundreds of green eyes, and, the <u>implied</u> metaphor of fireflies stitching the night as if they were sewing it.

f. How does the poet connect the earth and sky?

   Pale threads of light.

 *Exercise*

WRITE A POEM ABOUT YOUR LIFE.

 *Exercise*

WRITE A POEM ABOUT YOUR SPOUSE.

 *Exercise*

WRITE A POEM ABOUT YOUR CHILDREN.

 *Exercise*

WRITE A POEM ABOUT YOUR MOTHER.

 *Exercise*

WRITE A POEM ABOUT YOUR FATHER.

 *Exercise*

WRITE A POEM ABOUT THE PERSON YOU LOVE MOST.

 *Exercise*

WRITE A POEM ABOUT A GREAT RELATIONSHIP IN YOUR LIFE.

 *Exercise*

WRITE A POEM ABOUT YOUR FEELINGS TOWARD GOD.

 *Exercise*

WRITE A POEM ABOUT SOMEONE OR SOMETHING YOU
DISLIKE OR FEAR.

DISCUSSION QUESTIONS ABOUT THE POETRY EXERCISE:

1. If you gave each poem a color what color would you give it and why?

2. What emotion best describes the poem?

3. What phrase in the poem best describes the poem?

4. Would you want anybody else to see this poem?

    If so, who would you show it to?

5. Was it hard or easy to write this poem? Why?

LISTEN

When I ask you to listen to me and you start giving
advice,
you have not done what I asked.
When I ask you to listen to me and you begin to tell me
why
I shouldn't feel that way, you are trampling on my
feelings.
When I ask you to listen to me and you feel you have to
do
something to solve my problems, you have failed me,
strange
as that may seem.
So please, just listen and hear me. And if you want to talk,
wait a few minutes for your turn and I promise I'll listen
to you.

The bridge of I CAN

The Bridge of I CAN represents another stage which figures prominently in the journey, as you make your departure from *Someday I'll*. In fact, this bridge may seem to loom larger than the one you've crossed already. Here is where, with a more sure-footed stance, you begin to garner the determination that you can make choices about your life.

For many of us, **The Bridge of I CAN** is a tricky one to cross over! While the previous **Bridge of I AM** helped us to pinpoint who we believe we are and what is important to us, it now becomes necessary to believe we have the ability to effect that which is important to us. The question becomes, "I know who I am and I know what I want, but do I really believe I can make it happen?"

This may range from making choices in relationships, a decision regarding non-productive behavior, a desirable attitude adjustment or revamping your responses and reactions to day-to-day occurrences. For instance, you may want to explore a past conflict which presently impacts your life.

For instance, in your childhood, you may have thought your care-giver(s) favored a sibling or another child who also lived in the domicile over you. Your learned response could have been to misbehave in order to get attention. Learned behaviors, positive and non-productive behaviors, tend to stick with us over the years. Do you ever catch yourself behaving inappropriately ~ knowing better, but thinking that "any attention is better than NO attention!"

Another example: Remember high school? Maybe you didn't make the varsity team, the cheerleader squad or the debate club? Or maybe you feel you were excluded because you simply did not 'fit' into a certain group you wanted to be part of? Was your response, as a result, to be hesitant toward subsequent efforts to engage yourself in new involvement? Today, you may shy away from asking for that promotion, or that pay-hike, because you either feel you do not deserve it, or fear being rejected so you choose to not try.

There are many, many examples of present-day behaviors which are but reflections of 'survival skills' learned in the past. Not trying ~ for fear of failure ~ may seemingly save hurt feelings. But shielding one's self from 'hurt feelings' often means also shielding one's self from life's joys! The good news is that **The Bridge Of I CAN** is ready for you to cross at any time, and *Learning Self-Therapy Through Writing* will help you safely to the other side! Now. Are you ready to cross over?

The following two-part exercise should help you to clarify some thoughts and feelings you have about some changes you want to make in your life. You may want to think about which parts of it you want to share with the group, and which parts you wish to commit to your journal. Further, it may be that you'll want to discuss parts with a member of the *Learning Self-Therapy Through Writing* facilitation team. Whichever you decide, as always, it will be most beneficial to be completely frank in your responses.

 *Exercise Part One*

Please reflect for a few moments then respond to these questions. Please be very frank. Try to use two-to-three sentences in each of your responses. Some answers you may be willing to share with others in the group; some you want to discuss with a member of the *Learning Self-Therapy Through Writing* team; or you may choose to broach some of the subjects in your personal journal.

1. What would you like to see move more quickly in your life?

2. What would you like to see move more slowly, thoroughly and thoughtfully?

3. What would you like to understand better about yourself?

4. What would you feel good about if it happens?

5. What would you feel bad about if it happens?

Exercise Part Two

__Refer to your answers in__ _Exercise part one_ __as you respond:__

1. (a) List three things you have not yet done to make this move more quickly.

    (b) List three things you CAN do to make this move more quickly.

2. What CAN you do to assure this matter is carefully and thoughtfully dealt with?

3. How CAN you be more effective in learning what does and does not motivate you?

4. What CAN you do to accommodate making this happen so you can feel good?

5. What CAN you do to prevent this from happening so you won't feel badly?

Congratulations!

You are working your way across
The Bridge of I CAN!

DON'T BE FOOLED BY ME

Don't be fooled by me.
Don't be fooled by the face I wear,
For I wear a thousand masks, masks that I'm afraid to take off, and none of them are me.
Pretending is an art that's second nature with me, but don't be fooled, for God's sake, don't be fooled.

I give the impression that I'm secure, that all is sunny and unruffled with me, within as well as without, that
confidence is my name and coolness is my game; that the water's calm and I'm in command, and that
      I need no one.
But don't believe me.
Please.

My surface may seem smooth, but my surface is my mask.
Beneath this lies no complacence.
Beneath dwells the real me in confusion, in fear, and aloneness,
But I hide this. I don't want anybody to know it.
I panic at the thought of my weakness and fear of being exposed.
That's why I frantically create a mask to hide behind, a nonchalant, sophisticated facade, to help me pretend,
      to shield me from the glance that knows.
But such a glance is precisely my salvation. My only salvation.
And I know it. That is if it's followed by acceptance, if it's followed by love. It's the only thing that will assure
      me of what I can't assure myself, that I am worth something.

But I don't tell you this. I don't dare. I'm afraid to.
I'm afraid you'll think less of me, that you'll laugh at me, and your laugh would kill me.
I'm afraid that deep-down I'm nothing, that I'm no good, and that you will see this and reject me.
So I play my game, my desperate game, with a facade of assurance without, and a trembling child within.
And so begins the parade of masks. And my life becomes a front.

I idly chatter to you in the suave tones of surface talk. I tell you everything that is really nothing, and nothing
      of what's everything, of what's crying within me; so when I'm going through my routine do not be
fooled by what I'm saying. Please listen carefully and try to hear what I'm not saying, what I'd like to
be able to say, what for survival I need to say, but what I can't say.

I dislike hiding. Honestly!
I dislike the superficial game I'm playing, the phony game.
I'd really like to be genuine and spontaneous, and me, but you've got to help me. You've got to hold out your
      hand, even when that's the last thing I seem to want.
Only you can wipe away from my eyes the blank stare of breathing death.

Only you can call me into aliveness. Each time you're kind and gentle, and encouraging, each time you try to
      understand because you really care, my heart begins to grow wings, very small wings, very feeble
      wings, but wings. With your sensitivity and sympathy, and your power of understanding, you can breathe
      life into me.
      I want you to know that.
I want you to know how important you are to me, how you can be the creator of the person that is me if you
choose to.
Please choose to. You alone can break down the wall behind which I tremble, you alone can remove my mask.
      You alone can release me from my shadow-world of panic and uncertainty, from my lonely person.
Do not pass me by. Please...do not pass me by.

It will not be easy for you. A long conviction of worthlessness builds strong walls.
The nearer you approach me, the blinder I strike back.
I fight against the very thing I cry out for.
But I am told that love is stronger than walls, and in this lies my hope.
Please try to tear down those walls with firm hands, but with gentle hands, for a child is very sensitive.
Who am I, you may wonder. I am someone you know very well.
For I am every man you meet, and I am every woman you meet.

Author Unknown

The bridge of I WANT TO

The Bridge of I WANT TO represents another stage which figures prominently in the journey as you make your departure from *Someday I'll*. In fact, this Bridge is always on our minds, yet taking action and actually crossing over is quite another story! Not to worry! The key to crossing **The Bridge of I WANT TO** is learning to internalize and clarify exactly what it is you want to do, or change, or feel, or say, or think, or learn – and developing the wherewithal to accomplish it!

To begin with, it is necessary to determine your goals. This is the only way to be clear about what it is you want to do once you cross the bridge. In approaching **The Bridge of I WANT TO,** be sure to bring along your goals outline – which means spending a little time defining what your goals are. There are some specific things to know about goals and goal-setting. Note what each goal-definition means to you.

1. Goals must be realistic

2. Goals should be specific

3. Goals should be measurable

4. Goals should have objectives with timelines

5. Goals can be short and long-term

A trap many of us encounter in goal attainment is that once we've reached a goal, we fail to reset new goals. When this happens, feelings of 'slippage' or lack of progress can feel overwhelming. Remember, as you set goals for your life, it is wise to do so in stages, so that you are not likely to feel stuck and unproductive.

Many times, goals can come in stages. For instance, an initial goal might be to return to school. Once that is achieved, a goal could be to achieve high marks in coursework. As that becomes reality, the goal then elevates to seeking certification, a diploma or degree. The key is to set your goals with an eye always toward your future – meaning more goals and more goals and more goals!

Goal-setting Exercise

Below, list five goals in your life at this time. To get started, you might want to use "completing my *Self-Therapy Through Writing* course" as a goal. This means you may include some issues you want to specifically address; how long you plan to spend working on a specific issue; how you will know that you are progressing; and whether it is a long or short term goal. The following examples may be helpful as you begin your goal-setting:

GOAL	Specific	Short-term Objectives	Long-term	Timelines
New job	Computer technician	resumes; phone contacts; trade mags; cover letters; in 6 weeks	3 interviews	new job 4 mos.
Vacation	Paris	price checks; basic French; hotels; library for hot-spots; plan itinerary; 4 weeks	tickets; house sitter; mail & TIMES hold sched. 2 wks.	Mar. or June

Writing Exercise

You have by now hopefully decided to step toward the other side of ***The Bridge of I CAN***. As you review your goals, <u>select one of them and write a short story</u>. In this case, the story should be 'futuristic', and focused on how you moved from wishing that you could meet your goal, to actually achieving it! What you will do is engage in visualization. Later in the course, we will discuss the process of visualization in more depth, as there are structured methods you can use to realize your goals. Please feel free to be candid and creative as you tell the tale of how you progressed as you worked toward 'goal attainment'. At the same time, try to include enough realism so that your story of goal attainment can be inspirational to you!

Remember ~

"A GOAL
not written
is simply a wish"

My Story

My Story, continued

Success Through Visualization

Visualization is simply a technique of imagining things the way you want them to be. Visualization is the process of using your imagination to help you achieve goals and make changes in your life. Many experts ~ both in the social and the psychological sciences ~ believe the power of the imagination exceeds the power of the will.

You have probably heard the adage, "we are what we think". Thinking sad thoughts makes us feel unhappy. Likewise, imagining positive scenes can help us to relax and feel happy. The famous psychologist, Carl Jung, frequently referred to visualization as the use of active imagination.

Visualization is a natural process. Daydreams, memories and wishes are ways to picture what we want. Visualization works because our subconscious mind believes whatever we say or think is actually the truth. It operates based on our dominant or most prevalent thoughts.

Visualization is like watching an original movie in your mind that is written, directed and produced by **YOU**. The ideas and dreams that you have in your mind can be turned into something real that takes shape in your everyday life.

There are several steps to take in learning how to visualize properly so that you can bring about the specific end results that you desire.

On the following page are four steps which you can use to begin your process of visualization. It is hoped that as you continue *Learning Self-Therapy Through Writing*, you can develop your own methods of engaging visualization as a way to move toward goal achievement.

Exercise in Visualization

STEP 1

Think of something that you want to do successfully. Write a brief statement about it.

STEP 2

Get a clear picture of yourself successfully completing the activity. Write about that picture. What are you doing in it? Is anyone else present? Where are you?

STEP 3

Sit quietly with your eyes closed and focus on this picture until it is crystal clear. Write about what you have just seen in your mind's eye.

STEP 4

Visualize this picture three times daily until the change begins to occur. What can you do in the process to advance that change?

Exercise to Refresh Your Goals

Remember the Goal-setting exercise you logged into your workbook recently? This is a refresher ~ a reminder that setting goals prepares you for a successful future. Learning the rules of goal-setting will give you more knowledge about how to set goals properly. The following recommendations tie in your goal-setting activities with the visualization process.

1.   Always write down your goals, and focus on what you want to happen!

2   Make your goals exciting, and picture yourself in action!

3.   Set some short-term and long-term goals, and imagine yourself accomplishing them one-by-one.

4.   Make your goals specific, and create mental themes around them!

5.   Once you achieve your goal in a particular area, immediately set a new target in that area ~ and imagine.

The following page is for you to reproduce. The Weekly Goals Sheet will give you something tangible to mark your progress, as you make your way across **The Bridge of I CAN.**

Weekly Goals Sheet

GOAL	Specific	Short-term Objectives	Long-term	Timelines

The Bridge of I WANT TO is the third one you will cross in your departure from *Someday I'll.* This Bridge leads you onto solid ground. You will discover yourself to be far away from that nebulous place where procrastination, ambiguity, self-doubt, shame, fear and a host of other unproductive feelings haunt you.

You have discovered many things about who you are by crossing over **The Bridge of I AM.** You have discovered your many strengths as you continued your journey over the esteem-building expanse, called **The Bridge of I CAN,** and now it is time to make a decision that leads you a step further ~ to the place where your determination blossoms and prepares you for action!

The challenges and barriers to getting off *Someday I'll* are not simple ones, and may well involve issues you have floundered with for much of your adult life. But you see that it can be done. You believe that it can be done. It is hoped that you by now WANT to make the life-changes, clearing away the issues you believe have hampered your spiritual, personal, professional and emotional progress in the past.

You have learned to Visualize ~ to picture yourself where you want to be, doing what you would like to be doing, and behaving in ways you know work best for growth and success. One way to help make decisions that are healthy for you is to believe in yourself, and believe you deserve positive end results. This is often referred to as 'affirming' oneself. Affirming is a process through which you write sentences about the way you want to feel about yourself, and how you want things to be for yourself. These sentences are called *Affirmations.* They are used to program new beliefs into the sub-conscious data bank. It is best to put this style of 'positive self-talk' into the present tense. Some examples are:

I am a good student because I enjoy learning.

I am feeling great because I exercise at least four times each week.

My writing is improving and I spend one hour daily writing.

How do affirmations relate to your safely crossing over **The Bridge of I WANT TO?** What does visualization have to do with crossing over **The Bridge of I WANT TO?** Consider this: Seeing yourself as you want to be and telling yourself you are capable of becoming the person you dream of being are stepping-stones to reality.

There are several general rules for writing affirmations. After you review those rules listed on the following page, you will begin to see that you truly can achieve that which you can conceive. Further, you will begin to see that you <u>want to!</u>

Rules for Writing Affirmations:

Use the here and now -
Write the affirmation as if your are already doing that which you desire to accomplish.

Keep it real -
Write affirmations that are realistic to you here and now. Don't set yourself up for failure. Know it, write it, and do it.

Write what you want -
Write affirmations that state what you want and not what you don't want.

It's about you -
Write affirmations about you and not about others.

Paint a picture -
Write affirmations that paint word pictures for you. Your words should be full of action and power.

Beware if you share -
Write affirmations that are only for you. If you share them, share only with people who will encourage you and not the "it can't be done crowd."

After you have written your affirmations, read them everyday. Read them with power and work at them with passion.

Good affirmations start with words such as:

I control my...
I am personally accountable for...
I take great pride in...
I have a positive...
I enjoy...
I believe in...

BE AS SPECIFIC AS POSSIBLE!

My Affirmations

WHEN WE WERE IN LOVE

Once upon a long ago when we were so in love,
        It seemed we'd never be apart, we're meant like hand in
        glove.
But years play tricks upon the young, and suddenly we're old,
        And though we love each other still, the fires of youth are
        cold.
The loving patience that we had is now in short supply,
        And keeping peace between us now is something we don't
        try.
The secret conversations we would have when night was deep,
        All about our hopes and dreams; and love instead of sleep.
We used to give each other comfort, sweet when we were sad,
        And face the world as man and wife; together things
        weren't bad.
But now our secret selves are hidden far away inside,
        Our little world of lovers young has withered up and died.
And though I'll love you always dear, it's not the same to me,
        Through all the lonely years ahead, apart we'll have to be.

Anonymous

Congratulations! You have crossed three Bridges in your quest to leave behind *Someday I'll.* You conquered **The Bridge of I AM, The Bridge of I CAN, and The Bridge of I WANT TO.** It is now time for that final crossing ~

The bridge of I'LL DO IT TODAY

This means it is time to sum up and put into action all of the parts that make you a complete and self-actualized person.

Recall, if you will, that the first crossing, **The Bridge of I AM,** provided opportunities to peek through the windows of your past; to gain some insight about why you became the person you are. Starting out may have been the most challenging part thus far, because it probably included painful thoughts and acknowledgements, and dredged up memories you have worked hard to leave behind. However, by now you know that until issues are faced head-on, they will remain unresolved. Unresolved issues prompt us to act-out in unproductive ways that we cannot explain or seem to stop!

The Bridge of I CAN helped you to realize that attitudes and behaviors can and do change, but only when we work at making those changes. This is the point at which we decide that we are, after all, capable of making the life-changes that can lead to the types of lives we want to live. We come to know that there are few things we cannot improve upon, if only we are willing to give issues the attention necessary. By now, you have probably also decided that you can design your life the way you want to, measured only by the amount of effort you are willing to put toward the goal!

Crossing over the **Bridge of I WANT TO** brings about progressively growing self-confidence that whatever you can envision for yourself is indeed doable ~ again, provided you are willing to put in the work necessary to accomplish your missions. To *WANT* to achieve a goal, once you've realized that indeed you *CAN* achieve that goal, leaves only the plan of ACTION! You are now poised to begin your journey across that final leg ~ ***The Bridge of I'LL DO IT TODAY!***

As you being this journey into making dreams, wishes and goals become realities, pay close attention to the pitfalls that can snare you as you make this final trek. For instance, it is easy to tell yourself, "I am sticking with my goals. I have simply delayed the timelines a bit .... hey, I'll get it done sometime!"

Certainly there are instances when reasons for putting off goal-attainment seem logical, and they may be. There can be illness, job issues, family-related events; and a host of rational justifications. Just take stock that you are not slipping into old habits! If not vigilant, you might find yourself headed back toward that place you have worked hard to escape. Remember that self-defeatist place ~ *Someday I'll ?*

The Bridge of I'LL DO IT TODAY deals with a bug-a-boo that haunts practically everyone at some point in their lives. It is **procrastination!** Sometimes procrastination can mean putting off until tomorrow what you can do today, or it can mean putting off until next week – next month – next year – next millennium that which can be done today! Let us be clear on what the term means.

Webster's New World Thesaurus lists these words along with procrastination: drag, linger, trail, poke, dally, tarry, dawdle, loiter. It also says "... to proceed in a dilatory fashion." What are some words you use for 'procrastination'?

Sometimes we miss opportunities because our past learning styles keep us from seeing certain things that are right in our paths. We develop blind spots to new opportunities because they don't fit our perceptions of the way things are. And all too often, we put off and put off that which we could do today. *Learning Self-Therapy Through Writing* will help you learn to eliminate some of the excuses, reasons, rationales, justifications and explanations we often use, which impede growth and success.

You may want to take this time to evaluate your own personal values. What we place the most importance on is often what gets most of our attention. The mini-evaluation checklist on the next page will help you recognize what you really consider important as you review the list of words. Each of them ~ honesty, friendship, freedom ~ has a certain value attached to it. That value is subjective, based on individual perceptions of what is important to you.

The exercise has two parts. Once your values list is complete, please respond to the questions for discussion.

Personal Values Checklist

Rank the following words in the order which you feel is the most important to the least important in your life. (1-most / 15-least)

_____ Marriage

_____ Money

_____ Friends

_____ Security

_____ Freedom

_____ Family

_____ Education

_____ Honesty

_____ Travel

_____ Job

_____ Religion

_____ Community Involvement

_____ Car

_____ Pride & Dignity

_____ Fame

Discussion Questions
for Personal Values Checklist

1. If you had to eliminate all but five of the items on the list, which five would you keep?

2. If you had to take an educated guess at the five personal values most people in your country would choose, which ones do you think they would keep?

3. How consistent are your core values with your present life-style?

Creative Journal Keeping

As you progress in **Learning Self-Therapy Through Writing,** you will discover that creative journal-keeping is a therapeutic tool which promotes opportunities for self-understanding ~ and language skills development through writing. The Creative Journal Method nurtures self-esteem while strengthening communication skills. Creative Journaling helps to develop the imagination and creative expression, and encourages clarity for successful self-examination and concentration.

Journal entries constitute one's private thoughts and may be recorded in any fashion the writer chooses. In this course, however, some subject matter has been considered for you. The topic areas have been carefully designed to aid you in your self-journey. There will be times during which you may choose to write without direction - simply jotting down any flow of ideas. At other times, you will note a sequence and process which has been selected to help stimulate your own creativity as you hone your writing skills.

There are two primary objectives in *Learning Self-Therapy Through Writing.* One is to sharpen your present writing skills and develop new ones; and the other is to mesh these skills with individualized explorations of your 'self'. By implementing the Self-Therapy Model customized for this coursework, the combination of self-inventory and creative writing can lead to more prosperous and happy lives!

So ~ prepare to move through the next several weeks with an open mind, a willing heart, and a determined spirit! May your life goals be attained!

Creative Journal-Keeping

As you progress in Learning Self-Therapy Through Writing, you will discover that creative journal-keeping is a therapeutic tool for gaining self-understanding and practicing language skills through writing. The Creative Journal Method nurtures self-esteem while strengthening communication skills. It develops imagination and creative abilities as well as concentration and clarity.

Journal entries constitute one's private thoughts and may be recorded in any fashion the writer chooses. Many maintain journals in the same way they log daily activities in their diaries. However, Creative Journal-Keeping fosters a deeper intent. As a result of *Learning Self-Therapy Through Writing,* you will discover journaling methods and concepts that help you keep track of your 'inner life'.

The benefits of journaling are numerous. When you journal consistently, you will discover the abilities to:

- feel comfortable writing

- express feelings and thoughts

- acquire the habit of self-reflection and self-expression

- learn to communicate experience in words

- become more observant of yourself and others

- foster a positive self-concept

- exercise imagination and innate talent

- strengthen attention span and ability to focus

- enrich language and art skills through regular practice

- develop a greater sense of self-responsibility

- use both visual and verbal processes (right and left brain)

- find resources and wisdom within

Journaling is creative and confidential, and unless you invite others to read or hear your journal entries, there is no chance of its content being critiqued or graded. You may wish to maintain a dual-journal system. This is where you write entries which you are willing to share with group members, the other will be strictly for your eyes only. In some classes where the art of journaling is used, a completely separate journal is kept.

The Value
of
Journal-Keeping

PRIVACY

The journal is a safe place to express yourself, because it is private and confidential. It provides practice in communication free from judgement, ridicule or failure.

RELAXATION

You can relax with your journal and get your thoughts and feelings out on paper without having to analyze or edit the work.

SPONTANEITY

Since it is not being done for performance or external scrutiny, journal work encourages honest expression and spontaneity. This opens up the writer's innate intuition and creativity.

INTEGRITY

The privacy of the journal fosters integrity and honesty with oneself. Since it is not intended for others to see, the journalist is communicating with her/himself. This is like looking in a mirror.

EXPERIMENTATION

The absence of pressure to perform or compete with others makes the journal a safe place to experiment with written language and art and to discover things that haven't been done before. This is a key element in the creative process. Since the pages of the journal are blank, whatever emerges is of the writer's own making!

GATHERING IDEAS

The journal is an excellent place to record creative ideas and make notes for use in developing more formal 'public' writing such as letters and essays.

IMAGINATION AND CREATIVITY

The integration of writing in the Creative Journal method stimulates imagination, creativity and originality. It fosters a respect for innovation, brainstorming, and applying new ideas. Creative Journaling also develops observation and self-expression skills.

VERBAL AND NON-VERBAL EXPRESSION

Creative Journaling helps less verbal individuals, as well as those with higher language skills, through simply providing practical writing.

RIGHT BRAIN DEVELOPMENT

Journal exercises in drawing, which are often a component of journaling, stimulate thinking and perceiving (right brain processes), which are often ignored in traditional modes of instruction. This is especially helpful to individuals whose learning or cognitive style is characteristically nonverbal.

LEFT BRAIN DEVELOPMENT

Consistent journaling ~ which is a part of *Learning Self-Therapy Through Writing* ~ encourages verbal (left-brain processes) development. As words are written in your journal, you are naturally mastering more comprehension and expression through regular practice.

EMOTIONAL BALANCE

Because of its confidential nature, the journal provides an unthreatening place to release feelings and pent-up emotions that may not have other outlets. Journaling fosters an acceptance of those feelings and consequently, of the self.

SELF-UNDERSTANDING

Spontaneous and reflective writing make Creative Journal exercises excellent tools for learning about oneself. Honesty and spontaneity set the stage for gaining insight into personal experience.

Creative Journaling

 Exercise

Journal work is especially helpful during times of crises or major changes. Now that you know some values of Creative Journaling, examine and discuss the following scenarios in which this specialized form of writing can be beneficial. Have you experienced any of them recently?

family crises

moving

changing jobs, schools, churches

addition of a new family member

death of a loved one

divorce or separation

illness or injury

conflict with others

personal revelations

A Very Special Person Has Chosen Success!

I want to begin this journal describing who I am and what is important to me.

I want to write about a person who had a huge impact on my life. Here I'll describe things we did together, some of our favorite things.

The best time I have ever had in my life was........

The most difficult time I have ever had in my life was........

Three things I remember that happened to me that I will never forget are.....

When I think of those three things today, I feel ....

The greatest loss I have ever experienced was when ....

When I experienced that loss, I remember how it made me want to ......

Now I will write about a significant other in my life, one that probably has a lot to do with the person I am today.

Why do I think that person affects me so deeply?

I think I will draw a picture of me and three important people in my life. I will write two things to indicate what is special about our relationships.

Now I will write a poem that tells how I feel most of the time, and I will be very honest so that it will count!

The holiday I consider most special
is _____.
Here's why I feel that way.

If I could change something about how I
celebrate that time, it would be this:

I will write about the event that caused me more pain in my life than any other. I will be gentle with myself when I recall the hurt I felt.

There are two individuals I wish I never had to see again. I want to write about them, and I have the right to be as candid or as rude as I want as I write in my journal!

I would like to write about the perfect relationship, one that I would be willing to work hard to get and to maintain.

I am going to write about the closest relationship I have at this time.

I will now list the people in my immediate family, and also write about how our relationships are most of the time.

My life is important. I have many things to look forward to in my future. Some of my expectations and plans include ....

To reach those goals, I am currently........

Things I was not aware of before, but which am aware of now, include .....

I have had some very strange dreams, and some that are very pleasant. The oddest one that scared me was about ....

I think I'd say my favorite dream is the one where ......

Once when I was hurt so badly I thought I could not go on. I am going to write about that right now.

If I could change something in my life at this moment for the better, I am sure it would be what I am going to tell about on this page.

Sometimes I believe there is injustice in the world, and I believe that I have been the victim of that injustice, especially when ......

There is one thing I would love to tell someone, and when I am able to do so, here is WHO and WHAT it would be!

The main things I hope to accomplish from Learning Self-Therapy Through Writing are ....

I must make a very important change in my life if I want to be happy. I will now write about what I have to do.

This is why I have not done it before now ....

Hatred and resentment are unproductive emotions that I want to rid myself of, and I will now examine why I have these intense feelings toward ......

ANYTHING IS POSSIBLE

If there was ever a time to dare,
to make a difference,
to embark on something worth doing,
IT IS NOW.
Not for any grand cause, necessarily...
but for something that tugs at your heart,
something that's your inspiration,
something that's your dream.

You owe it to yourself
to make your days here count.
HAVE FUN.
DIG DEEP.
STRETCH.

DREAM BIG.
Know, though, that things worth doing
seldom come easy.
There will be good days.
And there will be bad days.
There will be times when you want to turn around,
pack it up,
and call it quits.
Those times tell you
that you are pushing yourself,
that you are not afraid to learn by trying.

PERSIST.

Because with an idea,
determination,
and the right tools,
you can do great things.
Let your instincts,
your intellect,
and your heart,
guide you.

TRUST.

Believe in the incredible power of the human mind.
Of doing something that makes a difference.
Of working hard.
Of laughing and hoping.
Of lazy afternoons.
Of lasting friends.
Of all the things that will cross your path this year.

The start of something new
brings the hope of something great,
ANYTHING IS POSSIBLE.

A Special Section

especially for those affected

by drug or alcohol abuse

Twelve Steps of Recovery
from Narcotics Anonymous' Basic Text

1. We admitted we were powerless over our addiction - that our lives had become unmanageable.

2. We came to believe that a Power greater than ourselves could restore us to sanity.

3. We made a decision to turn our will and our lives over to the care of God as we understood Him.

4. We made a searching and fearless moral inventory of ourselves.

5. We admitted to God, to ourselves, and to another human being the exact nature of our wrongs.

6. We were entirely ready to have God remove our shortcomings.

7. We humbly asked Him to remove our shortcomings.

8. We made a list of all persons we had harmed and became willing to make amends to them all.

9. We made direct amends to such people wherever possible, except when to do so would injure them or others.

10. We continued to take personal inventory and when we were wrong promptly admitted it.

11. We sought through prayer and meditation to improve our conscious contact with God as we understood Him, praying only for the knowledge of His will for us and the power to carry that out.

12. Having had a spiritual awakening as a result of these steps, we tried to carry the message to addicts and to practice these principles in all our affairs.

Explain the Steps Simply

1. I need help - my life is a mess.

2. There is help available.

3. I'll get help.

4. Who and What am I?

5. What does someone else think?

6. Look at what is wrong with my life.

7. Ask what I can do to change.

8. Look at the damage I cause.

9. Begin to repair the damage.

10. Look at me each day for a change.

11. Continue asking for help.

12. Living a better way.

The Power of Prayer
or
When You're Almost Convinced Your Prayer Is Unheard

Have you ever felt the urge to pray for someone and then just put it on a list and said, "I'll pray for them later."? Or has anyone ever called you and said, "I need you to pray for me, I have this need."? Read the following story that was sent to me and may it change the way that you may think about prayer and also the way you pray. You will be blessed by this one.

A missionary on furlough told this true story while visiting his home church in Michigan...While serving at a small field hospital in Africa, every two weeks I traveled by bicycle through the countryside to a nearby city for supplies. This was a journey of two days and required camping overnight at the halfway point. On one of these journeys, I arrived in the city where I planned to collect money from a bank, purchase medicine and supplies, and then begin my two-day journey back to the field hospital.

Upon arrival in the city, I observed two men fighting, one of whom had been seriously injured. I treated him for his injuries and at the same time talked to him about the Lord Jesus Christ. I then traveled two days, camping overnight, and arrived home without incident.

Two weeks later I repeated my journey. Upon arriving in the city, I was approached by the young man I had treated. He told me that he had known I carried money and medicines. He said, "Some friends and I followed you into the country, knowing you would camp overnight. We planned to kill you and take your money and drugs. But just as we were about to move into your camp, we saw that you were surrounded by 26 armed guards." At this I laughed and said that I was certainly all alone out in that country campsite.

The young man pressed the point, however, and said, "No sir, I was not the only person to see the guards. My five friends also saw them, and we all counted them. It was because of those guards that we were afraid and left you alone." At this point in the sermon, one of the men in the congregation jumped to his feet and interrupted the missionary and asked if he could tell him the exact day that this happened. The missionary told the congregation the date, and the man who interrupted told him this story: "On the night of your incident in Africa, it was morning here and I was preparing to go play golf. I was about to putt when I felt that urge to pray for you. In fact, the urging of the Lord was so strong, I called men in this church to meet with me here in the sanctuary to pray for you. Would all of those men who met with me on that day stand up?"

The men who had met together to pray that day stood up. The missionary wasn't concerned with who they were - he was too busy counting how many men he saw. There were 26. This Story is an incredible example of how the Spirit of the Lord moves in mysterious ways. If you ever hear such prodding, go along with it. Nothing is ever hurt by prayer except the gates of hell. I encourage you to forward this to as many people as you know. If we all take it to heart, we can turn this world towards Christ once again. Have a great day!

THE POWER OF PRAYER as the above true story clearly illustrates, "with God all things are possible" and more importantly, how God hears and answers prayers of the faithful. After you read this, please pause and give God thanks for the beautiful gift of your faith, for the powerful gift of prayer, and for the many miracles He works in your own daily life.

Author Unknown

The Steps - Long Version

1. AWARENESS
   My life is messed up; I have tried everything I know and nothing helps. My life just keeps getting worse.

2. SEARCH
   There is help available out there someplace. I will find out who, what, and where it is and how I can become involved.

3. CONNECTING
   I will let all the resources know I need help straightening up my life and ask if and how they may be able to help.

4. INVENTORY
   I need to take a good look at me and my life and see what I need to work on so I quit tearing myself down.

5. SECOND OPINION
   Talk to someone else and find out if things are as bad as I think and if I am seeking the right kind of help.

6. WHAT I DON'T LIKE
   Look at what I feel needs to change about me and why.

7. CHANGE
   Begin to make changes in my behavior, attitudes, and actions with the helpful guidance of another.

8. DAMAGE
   Take a look at my behavior and actions and the damage and turmoil I have caused in my life as well as the lives of others.

9. REPAIR
   Work on cleaning up or repairing any damage or wreckage of my past life as soon as possible.

10. ME TODAY
    Keep check on my progress each day to see if I'm changing or working in the right direction for a better way of life.

11. CONTINUE USING HELP
    Stay in contact with help sources to deal with new situations as they arise.

12. LIVING A NEW LIFESTYLE
    Continue all that I have been doing - making changes in me, gaining knowledge and confidence in myself and others, beginning to trust myself and my decisions as well as trusting others to help me - all causing my life to get better and more enjoyable each day.

Of great assistance to me in understanding and accepting the need of HELP was the following poem:

Footprints in the Sand

Author - Anonymous

One night I had a dream.
I was walking along the beach with the Lord
and across the skies flashed scenes from my life.
In each scene I noticed two sets of footprints in the sand.
One was mine and one was the Lord's.
When the last scene of my life appeared before me,
I looked back at the footprints in the sand.
And to my surprise I noticed that many times
along the path of my life there was only one set of footprints.
And I noticed that it was at the lowest and saddest times in my life.
I asked the Lord about it,
"Lord, you said that once I decided to follow you, you would walk
with me all the way. But I noticed during the most troublesome
times in my life there is only one set of footprints.
I don't understand why you left my side when I needed you most."
The Lord said, "My precious child, I never left you
during your time of trial. When you see only one
set of footprints, I was carrying you."

At certain times in our lives, when things are really bad and we are unable to help ourselves, we need to be carried through if we are to make it. We need to have faith that someone else will help us. It's OK to allow others to do for us what we cannot do for ourselves. So long as I do what I can, when I can, for myself and don't depend upon others to do everything for me, I will continue to grow.

RELAPSE PREVENTION

It is critical to start focusing on Relapse Prevention as early as possible. The sooner started, the greater the chance of staying clean and sober. Also, the sooner new habits are developed, the more quickly and easily change will occur. Early on, one is very vulnerable and unaware of the little things that help or hinder. Enlist assistance to profile negative triggers; ask how to avoid them; and find out what to do if coming in contact with them unexpectedly. Then get help to list the positive triggers that will enable a clean and sober life and instructions on how to use them. Developing a good relapse prevention program as well as a structured daily routine will allow some organization to come into life.

The following are the basic suggestions for Relapse Prevention:

1)   Daily meetings.

2)   Daily talking to recovering addicts.

3)   Connection with a Higher Power.

4)   Knowing positive triggers and how to use them.

5)   Knowing negative triggers and what to do to avoid them.

6)   Regular talks with sponsor/inner support group.

7)   Enjoyment activity.

8)   Do something nice for one's self.

9)   Quiet time to reflect.

10) Good sleep habits.

11) Work on step work and self.

12) Set achievement goals schedule.

13) Allow TIME to make progress.

14) Expecting too much too soon will cause disappointment and loss of self-confidence.

15) Work on making new friends and improving family relationships.

RELATIONSHIPS

Learning What Friendship Is:

The caring and sharing of one's self with another without conditions.

Be careful not to lose focus on one's self in order to care for another.

One does NOT have to be in love to have sex. The lack of sex has led many people back out. If necessary, get laid and get rid of the urge and compulsion. Remember however, that today we strive not to hurt or use others. An honest, open discussion prior to sexual activities can avoid many unpleasant situations that may arise by compulsively rushing into or manipulating others to have sex.

Start every relationship with friendship. Proceed slowly and allow it to grow. Get guidance. Don't try to change another; work on one's self. Acceptance of each other's good and bad habits is the key to success. Neither person owns the other; lives are being shared.

PERSONAL HEALTH

Personal health is very important to a happy recovery. Being sick causes misery and discontent. If one feels good physically, one will be encouraged to work on mental and spiritual aspects of one's life, thus promoting "good" feelings in all aspects of one's recovery and a NEW way of living.

Suggestions:

1) Eat right
2) Exercise (supervised at the beginning)
3) Regular check-ups at the doctor/dentist
4) Hot bubble bath (on occasion) to relax mind and body
5) Meditation (to clear the mind)
6) Healthy Friendships
7) Activity with friends and peers
8) Quality time with family
9) Hobby
10) Get enough sleep
11) Keep One's Self in Check!

The New Footprints

Now imagine you and the Lord Jesus are walking along the beach together. For much of the way the Lord's footprints go along steadily, consistently, rarely varying in the pace.

But your prints are in a disorganized stream of zig zags, starts, stops, turnarounds, circles, departures, and returns. For much of the way it seems to go like this. But gradually, your footprints come in line with the Lord's, soon paralleling His consistently. You and Jesus are walking as true friends.

This seems perfect, but then an interesting thing happens; your footprints that once etched the sand next to the Master's are not walking precisely in His steps. Inside His large footprints is the smaller "sandprint," safely enclosed. You and Jesus are becoming one; again this goes on for many miles.

But gradually you notice another change. The footprints are black. This time it seems even worse than before. Zig zags all over the place. Stop...start. Deep gashes in the sand. A veritable mess of prints.

You're amazed and shocked. But this is the end of your dream. Now you speak: "Lord, I understand the first scene with the zig zags, fits, starts and so on. I was a new Christian, just learning. But You walked on through the storm and helped me learn to walk with you."

"That is correct," replied the Lord.

Then, when the smaller footprints were inside of Yours, I was actually learning to walk in Your steps. I followed You very closely."

"Very good. You have understood everything so far."

"Then the smaller footprints grew and eventually filled in with Yours. I suuppose that I was actually growing so much that I was becoming more like You in every way."

"Precisely."

"But this is my question, Lord. Was there a regression of something? The footprints went back to two, and this time it was worse than the first."

The Lord smiles, then laughs. "You didn't know?" He says, "That was when we danced."

Author Unknown

FOR HE WILL TURN YOUR MOURNING INTO DANCING!
Psalms 30:11

This next section is for

anyone who has been directly or indirectly

"touched" or hurt by drug or alcohol abuse.

WORKING WITH THOSE NEW IN RECOVERY

CHARACTERISTICS TO REMEMBER:

1) Newcomers have just lived in a totally physical world.
2) Newcomers trust and have confidence in no one, including themselves.
3) Newcomers are generally scared and confused.
4) Newcomers feel hopeless.
5) Newcomers don't really believe there is a way out, or that anyone is truly willing to help them at no charge.
6) Newcomers rarely know what they really want or need; they are basically lost in life.
7) NEVER say "If you use, you lose." Tell the Newcomer you'll be there for them whenever they need you, no matter what. Also that you truly care about them.
8) SPECIAL NOTE: Wording is very important. How something is said WILL make a difference. Think before you speak!

DEVELOPMENT PROCESS

Stage 1

1) Open up a Friendship: start out simple. Go for coffee and just talk in general. Let the newcomer bring up topics for discussion and let him know you're available to talk if he feels he needs to. Confidentiality is imperative. STAY POSITIVE: Don't find faults or point out problems you may see.

2) Agree with the Newcomer that his life may be messed up but point out it is not hopeless. Tell him you're willing to help him find new ways to straighten things.

3) Do NOT downgrade the Newcomer; find things to compliment. Begin to build his self-esteem and self-confidence. There are no failures, just people in need of guidance.

4) Begin Step Work. Discuss how once addicted and using, we are powerless to do anything about situations in life. Our thinking processes had shut down; only getting and using and finding ways and means of getting more had any importance. A negative outlook on life was the result, which in turn led to loss of any positive foresight which led to loss of interest, which led to loss of faith in ourselves and the world around us, and finally to loss of hope. Assist the new-comer in finding sources of help and indicate how each is of value. (Remember that Step 2 is not a spiritual step; spirituality has not yet become a part of the Newcomer's life.) Introduce the Newcomer to various sources of help; accompany him to AA/NA meetings; introduce him to people; make suggestions as to those whose recovery is sound.

Stage 2

1) Begin teaching spiritual concepts by relating physical situations to spiritual concepts:

Example 1:

Ask "What feelings would you have if I took you 10 miles out in the deepest, darkest woods I could find, told you to strip naked, and find your own way back?" (Expected answers would be "scared, lost, abandoned, confused, angry, alone".)
Translation: Coming into Recovery, you were in total darkness, lost and alone. You were "naked" because everything you had used to help all your life was taken from you, your skills and knowledge were no good to you. You need no longer stand in the woods alone. I'll be with you. I'll give you all you need to protect yourself and will show you the path out.

Example 2:

Ask "If I gave you a flashlight in the woods, where would you shine it? Behind you? Out ahead? Right in front of you?" Translation: Shine it behind you and you can't see where you're going. Out ahead, and you will stumble because you're not looking where you're walking. Shine it right in front of you and you'll have a fairly safe walk as you will see what is happening and where you are. (Note: Teach the newcomer that what may have been true in the past or might be in the future isn't necessarily the truth right now.)

Example 3:

Ask a guy to answer the following in his mind, not out loud to you, "How long is your penis?" His answer will most likely be the length when it is erect. Chances are, when you ask him it will not be erect. Therefore, it wasn't truth at the moment he was asked. (We addicts often do not see things and situations for what they really are. Not all situations are as bad as we think, nor will they turn out the way we think.)

At this point, faith in other humans may begin to bud; the newcomer may begin to understand we are trying to help. Trust will come later as the help the newcomer is receiving begins to show positive results. Faith in God may come much later.

2) Begin teaching how to focus thoughts.

Teach controlled daydreaming. (Use a physical picture of a place if the newcomer is unable to image one.) Have the newcomer focus being in that place: how it feels; what is seen; what is heard; what is smelled. Have him concentrate and see if any of the above are experienced.

This procedure helps to teach one to focus their mind on one thought, thus clearing the confusion of 60 thoughts going through the mind at once. It also enables a person to focus on one problem in life at a time instead of all his problems at once.

Stage 3

1) Spirituality is the coming into harmony with one's self, one's feelings and emotions and being at peace living in the real world. It does not have to include "GOD," though many do develop a faith in a "GOD" later. It is, however, not a requirement for recovery, serenity, or peace of mind; but it may help. Through spirituality and spiritual concepts I begin to understand why I react to situations like I do. I find it's OK to feel and have emotions and to let others know how I feel. I also begin to understand why other people are as they are and act as they do. Through spirituality, I develop trust and faith in myself and others.

2) Trust develops slowly, a little at a time. As an example, "You come to my home and I ask you for your coat; you trust me to return it to you when you are ready to leave. If I asked the same of your wallet, you probably would not give it to me. Later, maybe you buy a new pair of shoes that are too tight and you give them to me to have them stretched for you and bring them back a day or two later. Later, I may need to go somewhere and you trust me to use your car. Then you loan me money. Eventually, you trust me to hold your wallet while you go swimming.
Translation: At first, you tell me your name and maybe your phone number. Next, you share your problems in general (financial, work, etc.) then later more personal problems (love life, habits, etc.). After would probably follow some secrets from the past that are tearing you apart inside.

Stage 4

1) For a change to a better way of life, a Newcomer should be shown that by making changes, growth will occur.

   Suggestions:

   a) Most people get dressed in the same order every morning. Change the order in which clothes are put on.
   b) Before doing anything, ask, "Why is this being done?" and "Does it have to be done this way?"
   c) Every morning, the Newcomer should look in the mirror and say "I like me. I'm not perfect, but I'm OK today!"

2)   Work on changing attitudes. If respect is shown, it will also be received. Using good manners, things like "please" and thank you" can work wonders! "Mr.," "Ms.," and "Mrs." can also help at times. Ask for help; don't demand it. When suggestions are given, TRY them rather than just finding fault with them. Above all, DON'T SAY "I CAN'T" WITHOUT TRYING! Push it to the limit, then go one step further.

3)   A healthy mind won't live in a sick body for long; a sick mind will make a healthy body sick:

   Suggestions:

   a) Work on behavior changes.
   b) Keep one's word! Don't make commitments that can't (or aren't desired) be kept.
   c) Be on time.
   d) Take care of one's health as well as the mind.
   e) Pay bills on time.
   f) Learn to budget.
   g) Work on catching up old debts.
   h) Don't procrastinate. When something needs to be done, get started. Putting things off until later just results in more things needing to be done.

Stage 5

1)   BECOME A FRIEND:

   a) START with a handshake and introduce yourself.
   b) Don't expect anything from another person.
   c) Engage in conversation.
   d) Get to know one another.

2)   LEARN TO CARE ABOUT OTHERS

   a) Be interested in another's life.
   b) Help when asked.
   c) Be concerned about another's health and well-being.
   d) Help build another's faith and self-confidence.

3)   LEARN ABOUT LOVE: (What it is; How to Show It; How to Feel It)

   LOVE IS NOT SEX! Love is compassion and understanding, sharing pain and joy, opening one's heart, being there for another, helping another find peace and harmony, letting another help you back.

4) LEARN HOW TO HELP OTHERS WHILE STILL RECEIVING HELP ONE'S SELF:

a) Each person has experience and answers needed by the other.
b) By sharing experience and knowledge, each person gains by the warm feeling that comes with knowing one is helping another.

5) LEARN HOW TO LIVE AND ENJOY LIFE:

a) As changes occur, contentment occurs.
b) As problems are solved, self-confidence and self-esteem build.
c) As trust is received, trust will grow.
d) Attitude will become more positive.
e) As one starts to feel good, one will work harder to feel even better yet.

6) WORK ON RELAPSE PREVENTION:

a) What triggers ME wanting a drink/drug?
b) What helps ME not to use a drink/drug?
c) How should I schedule my day to benefit me most?
d) How can I get fast help?

Remember, relapse (and the behaviors surrounding it) begins long before actually picking up/using!

7) DEALING WITH PROBLEM SITUATIONS: FOCUS ON THE CAUSE, NOT THE PROBLEM! (OR THE 3R METHOD-REMOVE, REGROUP, RESOLVE/RETURN)

a) Remove one's self from the situation momentarily.
b) Regroup thoughts and regain clear thinking.
c) Resolve/Return with a positive plan of action to gain positive resolution.

As an example, assume one is angry at a friend. Determine first why?
a) My friend hurt me or someone I care about.
b) My friend is hurting himself; I care about my friend yet he won't listen to me.
c) My friend won't do what I want done.

Causes of anger in the above situation may be:

a) Hurt
b) Desertion
c) Physical Violence
d) Verbal Abuse
e) Abandonment
f) Feeling Trapped/Cornered
g) Misunderstanding
h) Confusion/Lack of Information
i) Fear

Determine WHY am I angry? Is my anger REALLY justified? What can I do to restore the friendship?

As a second example, assume that financial disaster is the problem. Possible causes are:

a) Irresponsibility
b) Poor (or no) Budgeting
c) Easy Credit
d) Spendthrift
e) Laziness (won't work)

Identifying which of the above is the CAUSE (or causes!) of the financial disaster is the beginning of the remedy.

8) All problems have an underlying cause; all can have a positive solution. A WILLINGNESS TO ACT is required - "I must look for the solution and work on it!" With time and practice, this process becomes easier, and remember, this is a program of progress, not perfection - go easy on one's self.

9) It is easy to say "I'll do (something)!" Doing it is the hard part. When something needs to be done, ask the newcomer if he is willing to do it, encourage him to start and keep encouraging him until he does. Monitor the progress, and if he falters or stops before completion, encourage him to stick with it until he has finished. He needs to prove to himself he can accomplish the task.

Assure the newcomer, and let him know that miracles don't necessarily happen right away. Seldom will he himself observe the change in his life as it happens over the short term. Assure him that things will get better.

NO MATTER WHAT, DON'T GIVE UP!!

TOOLS THAT HELP

SERENITY PRAYER

God, grant me the Serenity to accept
the things I cannot change,
the Courage to change the things I can, and
the Wisdom to know the difference.

Each morning, ask God for help to stay clean and to do the next right thing.

Each night, thank God for all He has given.

Tell someone you love them each day.

Tell yourself you love you too and that you're OK today.

Make yourself available to another even though you might think you have nothing to offer. They may think you do!

Look beyond recovering people and situations and become part of the real world. Socialize outside the fellowship with so-called "normal people". Get involved in the community, attend municipal meetings, join civic clubs, attend church, etc.

Accept people for who and what they are. Don't be prejudiced; everyone has something to offer. There is good in all people. Everyone deserves a chance to a better life. No one is hopeless. Remember, you were given a chance by others so pass it on.

Basic requirements for happiness are:
1) Roof over your head.
2) Food in your stomach.
3) Clothes on your back.
4) One (1) friend.
5) Something to believe in.

Basic requirements for Recovery:
1) A good sponsor.
2) Reading literature daily.
3) Talking to other Recovering people daily.
4) Daily prayer and meditation.
5) Daily 12-step meeting.

FINAL NOTES

1. Maintain confidentiality. If searching for help for someone, never reveal the person's name.

2. Never force someone to do something. Find ways to make him more comfortable accepting the need to do something. Forcing can do more damage than good in the long run.

3. When including others in discussion regarding helping another, obtain their permission first. Keep group as small as possible, including only people who have experienced the same situation. Then, if necessary, suggest the person work openly with the others. Not everything needs to be broadcast or discussed openly. Some things are personal and private and ought to stay that way.

4. Help the Newcomer to want to do things and to want to make changes. Don't make him feel he has to. (Like you, the Newcomer will only continue doing forced behavior so long as the gun is to his head. Take away the gun and reversion to old behavior will occur. When the Newcomer chooses to change behavior, he is more likely to maintain the change. Let him choose, not you.)

5. Let the Newcomer know he doesn't have to do anything in life provided he is willing to pay the consequences for his action. Reveal to him the consequences his actions have caused, and discuss if he is comfortable with them. Point out also whether or not he is following the suggestions given. Let the final choice be his.

6. Remember the Newcomer is only a misguided person looking for help. He is not trouble; he is not a burden; he is no different than each of us was at one time. Others had the patience to help us. Now it is our turn.

7. A newcomer is neither stupid nor undeserving. He may ask a lot of questions and need special attention.

8. No two people are exactly the same, so don't treat them that way. Each of us responds differently. (He is not you, and you are not he. Don't expect him to respond as you would. He needs time to grow.)

9. I must ask myself, "Who am I trying to impress with what I am doing? Myself? The person I'm trying to help?" (Answer - NEITHER!)

10. Share only experience and knowledge. Don't guess or share a suggestion in an area in which you know nothing. Tell the person "I don't know" or "I can't help you there" then help find someone who can.

THREE ANALOGIES

THE TITANIC

There are as many different addictions as there were seats on the luxury cruise ship Titanic. However, it didn't matter how many times you changed seats or which seat you sat in, the whole ship went down. Anyone that stayed on board went down with it no matter where they were sitting. Only those that got off the ship had a chance of surviving.

The same goes for switching addictions; it doesn't matter what you are addicted to, addiction will destroy you and your life. The only hope is to get out of addiction and learn to live life on life's terms in Recovery.

THE MAYFLOWER

Years ago, a group of people couldn't live the lifestyle they were living, so they chose to go to the New World and start a whole new way of life and living. However, as they crossed the ocean, the weather and seas got rough and some panicked, deciding to jump off the ship and swim, thinking they could make it back to where they came from. A few were rescued and pulled back onto the ship, but many weren't that lucky and drowned.

Even once they reached the New World, life wasn't perfect. They still had to work hard to build homes, plant crops, etc. They also had the responsibility of maintaining their new home and lifestyle.

If we look at Recovery, we find that we too can no longer live our old lifestyle and therefore set out to find a new one. The journey of the first year is tough and some panic and relapse. A few find their way back, others don't and die. Even once we get a foundation for our Recovery, we still have to maintain it by doing the right things we need to do One Day At A Time.

TWO NUNS

Two addicts should travel together for the same reason that two nuns travel together. One nun will make sure that the other nun doesn't get none.

One addict will spot the other addict's behavior and possibly prevent them from using (mostly out of jealousy, if I can't do it, I don't want you to).

THE COLD WITHIN

Six men trapped by happenstance
In dark and bitter cold.
Each one possessed a stick of wood,
Or so the story's told.

Their dying fire in need of logs
The first man held his back,
For on the faces around the fire
He noticed one was black.

The next man looking 'cross the way
Saw one not of his church,
And couldn't bring himself to give
The fire his stick of birch.

The third one sat in tattered clothes.
He gave his coat a hitch.
Why should his log be put to use
To warm the idle rich?

The rich man just sat back and
thought
Of the wealth he had in store.
And how to keep what he had earned
From the lazy, shiftless poor.

The Black man's face bespoke revenge
As the fire passed from sight.
For all he saw in his stick of wood
Was a chance to spite the white.

The last man of this forlorn group
Did naught except for gain.
Giving only to those who gave
Was how he played the game.

The logs held tight in death's still
hands
Was proof of human sin.
They didn't die from the cold without,
They died from the cold within.

Author Unknown

MONTHLY FLUSHING SESSIONS

❄ JANUARY____	⚘ MAY____	🏈 SEPTEMBER____
♥ FEBRUARY____	⚾ JUNE____	🎃 OCTOBER____
✿ MARCH____	⛵ JULY____	🍁 NOVEMBER____
☂ APRIL____	✺ AUGUST____	🎄 DECEMBER____

FLUSHING SESSION

1. Make a list of all your pressing issues, worries, concerns.

2. Make a list of possible solutions to address these issues, worries, and concerns.

Signed_____

Date_____

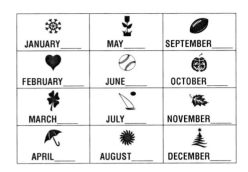

❄ JANUARY_____	🌷 MAY_____	🏈 SEPTEMBER_____
❤ FEBRUARY_____	⚾ JUNE_____	🎃 OCTOBER_____
🍀 MARCH_____	⛵ JULY_____	🍁 NOVEMBER_____
☂ APRIL_____	🌻 AUGUST_____	🎄 DECEMBER_____

FLUSHING SESSION

1. Make a list of all your pressing issues, worries, concerns.

2. Make a list of possible solutions to address these issues, worries, and concerns.

Signed_____

Date_____

❄ JANUARY_____	🌷 MAY_____	🏈 SEPTEMBER_____
♥ FEBRUARY_____	⚾ JUNE_____	🎃 OCTOBER_____
🍀 MARCH_____	⛵ JULY_____	🍁 NOVEMBER_____
☂ APRIL_____	✺ AUGUST_____	🎄 DECEMBER_____

FLUSHING SESSION

1. Make a list of all your pressing issues, worries, concerns.

2. Make a list of possible solutions to address these issues, worries, and concerns.

Signed_____

Date_____

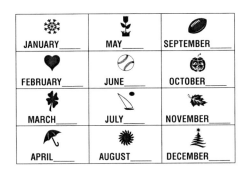

❄ JANUARY_____	🌷 MAY_____	🏈 SEPTEMBER_____
❤ FEBRUARY_____	⚾ JUNE_____	🎃 OCTOBER_____
☘ MARCH_____	⛵ JULY_____	🍁 NOVEMBER_____
☂ APRIL_____	✹ AUGUST_____	🎄 DECEMBER_____

FLUSHING SESSION

1. Make a list of all your pressing issues, worries, concerns.

2. Make a list of possible solutions to address these issues, worries, and concerns.

Signed_____

Date_____

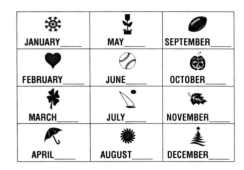

❄ JANUARY____	🌷 MAY____	🏈 SEPTEMBER____
♥ FEBRUARY____	⚾ JUNE____	🎃 OCTOBER____
🍀 MARCH____	⛵ JULY____	🍂 NOVEMBER____
☂ APRIL____	🌻 AUGUST____	🎄 DECEMBER____

FLUSHING SESSION

1. Make a list of all your pressing issues, worries, concerns.

2. Make a list of possible solutions to address these issues, worries, and concerns.

Signed_____

Date_____

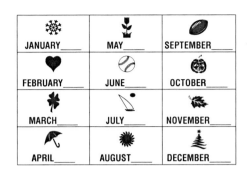

JANUARY____	MAY____	SEPTEMBER____
FEBRUARY____	JUNE____	OCTOBER____
MARCH____	JULY____	NOVEMBER____
APRIL____	AUGUST____	DECEMBER____

FLUSHING SESSION

1. Make a list of all your pressing issues, worries, concerns.

2. Make a list of possible solutions to address these issues, worries, and concerns.

Signed_____

Date_____

❄ JANUARY____	🌷 MAY____	🏈 SEPTEMBER____
❤ FEBRUARY____	⚾ JUNE____	🎃 OCTOBER____
☘ MARCH____	⛵ JULY____	🍂 NOVEMBER____
☂ APRIL____	☀ AUGUST____	🎄 DECEMBER____

FLUSHING SESSION

1. Make a list of all your pressing issues, worries, concerns.

2. Make a list of possible solutions to address these issues, worries, and concerns.

Signed_____

Date_____

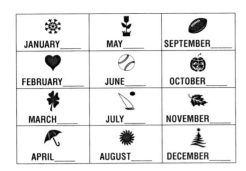

❄️ JANUARY_____	🌷 MAY_____	🏈 SEPTEMBER_____
❤️ FEBRUARY_____	⚾ JUNE_____	🎃 OCTOBER_____
🍀 MARCH_____	⛵ JULY_____	🍂 NOVEMBER_____
☂️ APRIL_____	🌻 AUGUST_____	🎄 DECEMBER_____

FLUSHING SESSION

1. Make a list of all your pressing issues, worries, concerns.

2. Make a list of possible solutions to address these issues, worries, and concerns.

Signed_____

Date_____

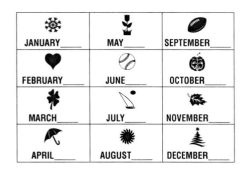

❄ JANUARY_____	⚘ MAY_____	🏈 SEPTEMBER_____
❤ FEBRUARY_____	⚾ JUNE_____	🎃 OCTOBER_____
☘ MARCH_____	⛵ JULY_____	🍁 NOVEMBER_____
☂ APRIL_____	✹ AUGUST_____	🎄 DECEMBER_____

FLUSHING SESSION

1. Make a list of all your pressing issues, worries, concerns.

2. Make a list of possible solutions to address these issues, worries, and concerns.

Signed_____

Date_____

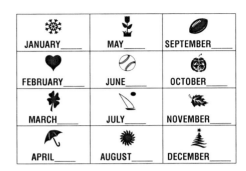

❄ JANUARY____	🌷 MAY____	🏈 SEPTEMBER____
❤ FEBRUARY____	⚾ JUNE____	🎃 OCTOBER____
🍀 MARCH____	⛵ JULY____	🍁 NOVEMBER____
☂ APRIL____	❃ AUGUST____	🎄 DECEMBER____

FLUSHING SESSION

1. Make a list of all your pressing issues, worries, concerns.

2. Make a list of possible solutions to address these issues, worries, and concerns.

Signed_____

Date_____

❄ JANUARY_____	⚘ MAY_____	🏈 SEPTEMBER_____
❤ FEBRUARY_____	⚾ JUNE_____	🎃 OCTOBER_____
☘ MARCH_____	⛵ JULY_____	🍁 NOVEMBER_____
☂ APRIL_____	✹ AUGUST_____	🎄 DECEMBER_____

FLUSHING SESSION

1. Make a list of all your pressing issues, worries, concerns.

2. Make a list of possible solutions to address these issues, worries, and concerns.

Signed_____

Date_____

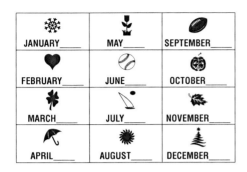

❄ JANUARY____	🌷 MAY____	🏈 SEPTEMBER____
❤ FEBRUARY____	⚾ JUNE____	🎃 OCTOBER____
☘ MARCH____	⛵ JULY____	🍁 NOVEMBER____
☂ APRIL____	☀ AUGUST____	🎄 DECEMBER____

FLUSHING SESSION

1. Make a list of all your pressing issues, worries, concerns.

2. Make a list of possible solutions to address these issues, worries, and concerns.

Signed_____

Date_____

SOMEDAY I'LL

There is an Island Fantasy
A "Someday I'll," we'll never see
When recession stops, inflation ceases
Our mortgage is paid, our pay increases
That someday I'll where problems end
Where every piece of mail is from a friend
Where the children are sweet and already grown
Where we all retire at forty-one
Playing backgammon in the island sun
Most unhappy people look to tomorrow
To erase this day's hardship and sorrow
They put happiness on "lay away"
And struggle through a blue today
But happiness cannot be sought
It can't be earned, it can't be bought
Life's most important revelation
Is that the journey means more than the destination
Happiness is where you are right now
Pushing a pencil or pushing a plow
Going to school or standing in line
Watching and waiting, or tasting the wine
If you live in the past you become senile
If you live in the future your on Someday I'll
The fear of results is procrastination
The joy of today is a celebration
You can save, you can slave, trudging mile after mile
But you'll never set foot on your Someday I'll
When you've paid all your dues and put in your time
Out of nowhere comes another Mt. Everest to climb
From this day forward make it your vow
Take Someday I'll and make it your Now!

WEEKLY CONTRACTS

MY WEEKLY CONTRACT WITH MYSELF

Week #_____

I_____ hereby make a binding commitment to complete the following task this week.

Task:

Barriers/fears I must address in order to complete this task:

1.

2.

3.

Signed_____

Date_____

MY WEEKLY CONTRACT WITH MYSELF

Week #_____

I_____ hereby make a binding
commitment to complete the following task this week.

Task:

Barriers/fears I must address in order to complete this task:

1.

2.

3.

Signed_____

Date_____

MY WEEKLY CONTRACT WITH MYSELF

Week #_____

I_____ hereby make a binding
commitment to complete the following task this week.

Task:

Barriers/fears I must address in order to complete this task:

1.

2.

3.

Signed_____

Date_____

MY WEEKLY CONTRACT WITH MYSELF

Week #_____

I_____ hereby make a binding commitment to complete the following task this week.

Task:

Barriers/fears I must address in order to complete this task:

1.

2.

3.

Signed_____

Date_____

BUILD A BETTER WORLD

"Build a better world," said God.
And I answered,
"How? The world is such a vast place,
And so complicated now,
And I am small and helpless,
There's nothing I can do."

But God in all His wisdom, said,
"Just build a better you."

Printed in the United States
102432LV00004B/110/A